Grammaropolis

PRESENTS

Meet the

Parts
of
Speech

8
POPULATION

Student Workbook

FIFTH GRADE

written by
THE MAYOR OF GRAMMAROPOLIS

HOUSTON

Edited by Christopher Knight
Cover and Interior Design by Mckee Frazior
Character Design by Powerhouse Animation

ISBN: 9781644420188
Copyright © 2020 by Grammaropolis LLC
Illustrations copyright © 2020 by Grammaropolis LLC
All rights reserved.
Published by Grammaropolis
Distributed by Six Foot Press
Printed in the U.S.A.

Grammaropolis.com
SixFootPress.com

Table of Contents

Table of Contents

For information on how Grammaropolis correlates to state standards, please visit us online at edu.grammaropolis.com.

FROM THE DESK OF THE MAYOR

There's a reason students can instantly recall everything that happened in their favorite movies but struggle to retain much of the important information you're trying to cover in school: people are hard-wired to remember what we connect with on an emotional level.

That's why grammar is so hard to teach. (As a former grammar teacher myself, I know firsthand.) Traditional materials are dry, abstract, and lifeless. There's nothing to connect with. Put simply, grammar is boring.

But it doesn't have to be! Our story-based approach combines traditional instruction with original narrative content, appealing to different learning styles and encouraging students to make a deeper connection with the elements of grammar.

In Grammaropolis, adverbs don't just modify verbs; adverbs are bossy! They tell the verbs **where** to go, **when** to leave, and **how** to get there. A pronoun doesn't just replace a noun; Roger the pronoun is a shady character who's always trying to trick Nelson the noun into giving up his spot.

And it works! Our mobile apps have already been downloaded over 2.5 million times, and thousands of schools and districts use our web-based site license. In other words, we don't skimp on the vegetables; we just make them taste good.

Thanks so much for visiting Grammaropolis. I hope you enjoy your stay!

– The Mayor

Meet the Parts of Speech!

Nouns

name a person, place, thing, or idea.

Verbs

express action or a state of being.

Adverbs

modify a verb, an adjective, or another adverb.

Adjectives

modify a noun or pronoun.

Prepositions

show a logical relationship or locate an object in time or space.

Pronouns

take the place of one or more nouns or pronouns.

Interjections

express strong or mild emotion.

Conjunctions

join words or word groups.

Grammaropolis

Meet the Nouns!

EXAMPLES

PERSON: <u>Mr. Jenkins</u> is the happiest <u>teacher</u> around.

PLACE: They went to <u>Oklahoma</u> for their field trip.

THING: There is a small <u>stack</u> of <u>pennies</u> on my <u>dresser</u>.

IDEA: We have all fought for <u>equality</u>.

Common Nouns and Proper Nouns

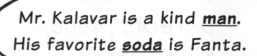

Mr. Kalavar is a kind **man**.
His favorite **soda** is Fanta.

Mr. Kalavar is a kind man.
His favorite soda is **Fanta**.

Pro Tip:
A noun that names a general person, place, thing, or idea is called a **common noun**.

Pro Tip:
A noun that names a specific person, place, thing, or idea is called a **proper noun**.

Let's Practice!

Instructions:
In each of the following sentences, circle any common nouns and underline any proper nouns.

EXAMPLE:
My cousin Wilson gave everyone in my class some chocolate from Belgium.

1. Laticia spent her afternoon at the park near her house.

2. Extra books are hard to come by at my school.

3. Dr. Pinky told me not to run very fast today.

4. We went to the doctor yesterday because we all felt queasy.

5. Someone should tell James not to steal things.

Your turn!

Instructions:
Write a sentence that includes at least one proper noun, a sentence that includes at least one common noun, and a sentence that includes at least one of each. Circle the common nouns and underline the proper nouns.

1. proper   _____

2. common   _____

3. one of each   _____

Concrete Nouns and Abstract Nouns

Pro Tip:
A **concrete noun** names a person, place, or thing that can be perceived by one or more of the five senses.

Pro Tip:
An **abstract noun** names an idea or quality that cannot be perceived by any of the five senses.

Let's Practice!

Instructions:
In each of the following sentences, circle any concrete nouns and underline any abstract nouns.

EXAMPLE:
My desire for relaxation led me to the most comfortable couch in the room.

1. When Ernie saw his neighbor riding a bike, he felt incredible envy.

2. As you get older, you will gain the freedom to eat more chocolate.

3. Daniela wrote such an amazing book!.

4. Sergei went to the store to buy a spare part for his bicycle.

5. Sometimes I think my dog has more intelligence than I do.

Your turn!

Instructions:
Write a sentence that includes at least one concrete noun, a sentence that includes at least one abstract noun, and a sentence that includes at least one of each. Circle the concrete nouns and underline the abstract nouns.

1. concrete _____

2. abstract _____

3. one of each _____

Collective Nouns

The **flock** of birds was so large that it almost blocked out the sun.

Jeremiah's scout **patrol** spends a lot of time on conservation projects.

Pro Tip:
A *collective noun* is a singular noun that names a group.

Let's practice!

Instructions:
Circle all of the collective nouns in the each of the following sentences.

EXAMPLE:
The largest ant colony ever discovered contained over 300 million ants.

1.   It was raining so hard that I could hardly see the rest of my team.

2.   Jaylen spent all day in school staring at a school of goldfish.

3.   If you want to be in a band, you have to practice.

4.   Felipe came home from the library with a bunch of books he'd already read.

5.   The loudest noise Kip ever heard was a herd of cattle stampeding toward him.

Your turn!

Instructions:
Use the collective nouns below to write your very own sentences.

1.   crowd   _____

2.   bouquet   _____

3.   stack   _____

Grammaropolis

Compound Nouns

Pro Tip:
A **compound noun** is formed when two or more words combine to make a single noun. A compound noun can be one single word, two words, or words connected by hyphens.

Let's practice!

Instructions:
Circle all of the compound nouns in each of the following sentences.

EXAMPLE:
Please tell Jack to come to the dining room for some watermelon.

1. Sasha asked the salesperson for more information.

2. After the thunderstorm ended, a ray of sunshine peeked through the clouds.

3. The runner-up in the sandcastle competition got to ride on the merry-go-round.

4. Neville begged his great-grandfather for another scoop of ice cream.

5. I have a thing against scarecrows.

Your turn!

Instructions:
Create your own compound nouns by adding another word to the words below.

cow	_____	ice	_____
dish	_____	key	_____
fire	_____	week	_____
day	_____	rule	_____

Singular Nouns and Plural Nouns

Singular Nouns:
I had a <u>dream</u> that I was being chased by a <u>wolf</u>.

Plural Nouns:
Why are <u>wolves</u> always chasing me in my <u>dreams</u>?

Pro Tip:
A **singular noun** names a single person, place, thing, or idea.
A **plural noun** names more than one person, place, thing, or idea.

Pro Tip:
Most nouns are made plural by adding -s, or -es to the singular form. The ones that don't are called **irregular** plural nouns.

Let's Practice!

Instructions:
In each of the following sentences, circle any singular nouns and underline any plural nouns.

EXAMPLE:

Jacoby knew that the same <u>rules</u> applied to all the <u>men</u>, <u>women</u>, and <u>children</u> on the boat.

1. No meal would be complete without hamburgers and ketchup.

2. I always run down dark hallways because I am afraid of ghosts.

3. Of all the children in the classroom, that child makes me laugh the most.

4. Charles dressed up as a wildebeest last year.

5. Gracia and her coworkers ordered a variety of cheeses from the waiter.

Your turn!

Instructions:
Turn the following singular nouns into plural nouns. Remember that some might be irregular!

shelf	_____	goose	_____
mailman	_____	baby	_____
glasses	_____	match	_____
person	_____	sheep	_____

Grammaropolis

Writing with Nouns

INSTRUCTIONS (PART ONE):
Brainstorm some of your favorite nouns for each of the following categories. Make different lists for action verbs that express physical action and action verbs that express mental action

PROPER	COMMON	ABSTRACT	COLLECTIVE	COMPOUND
-----------------	-----------------	-----------------	-----------------	-----------------
-----------------	-----------------	-----------------	-----------------	-----------------
-----------------	-----------------	-----------------	-----------------	-----------------
-----------------	-----------------	-----------------	-----------------	-----------------

INSTRUCTIONS (PART TWO):
Now choose TWO nouns from each of your categories and use them to write a short story. Don't forget to circle the nouns when you use them!

_____

_____

_____

_____

_____

_____

Grammaropolis

The Big Noun Quiz!

INSTRUCTIONS: Classify the noun type for the <u>underlined nouns</u> below from among the available options.

1.   The police <u>squad</u> surrounded the VIP for protection.

   O   abstract   O   collective   O   proper   O   compound

2.   The <u>cowbell</u> hanging from the doorway always rings when visitors arrive.

   O   abstract   O   collective   O   proper   O   compound

3.   All I ask is that you have a little <u>faith</u> in what we are doing.

   O   abstract   O   collective   O   proper   O   compound

4.   The restaurant went silent when my <u>teacup</u> shattered on the floor.

   O   abstract   O   collective   O   proper   O   compound

5.   We made plans to take <u>Spanish</u> at the local community college.

   O   abstract   O   collective   O   proper   O   compound

INSTRUCTIONS: Indicate whether the <u>underlined nouns</u> below are singular or plural nouns.

6.   That <u>sheep</u> is the smallest one I have ever seen!

   O   singular   O   plural

7.   You must have a lot of interesting <u>stories</u> to tell.

   O   singular   O   plural

8.   Yesterday the bus almost ran into a <u>herd</u> of cattle on the road.

   O   singular   O   plural

9.   One of the best things about living in Texas is being able to see <u>cattle</u> everywhere.

   O   singular   O   plural

10.   This book has been written exclusively with <u>children</u> in mind.

   O   singular   O   plural

Grammaropolis

Meet the Verbs!

I am an action verb!

I express action.

EXAMPLES

We **swam** in the river.
Juliet **accepted** her award.
Mohan **will speak** to the class.

I am a linking verb.

I express a
state of being.

EXAMPLES

Wilson's room **was** the cleanest.
Clowns **are** hilarious.
That chocolate milk **tastes** sour.

Action Verbs Express Action

Physical Action:
Francisco **caught** the ball!

Mental Action:
I **think** that I **know** the answer!

Pro Tip:
An action verb can express either **physical** action or **mental** action.

Let's practice!

Instructions:
Circle the action verb in each of the following sentences and indicate whether it is expressing physical or mental action.

EXAMPLE:

My grandfather (grew) a long, wispy goatee.   ___physical action___

1. Julie flew off the swing set.   _____

2. In Science class, we observe experiments closely. _____

3. Talia jogged across the street to the café on the corner. _____

4. Stobie wants a piece of chocolate cake.   _____

5. Gillian and her cousins pushed to the front of the line. _____

Your turn!

Instructions:
Write sentences using your own action verbs to express mental or physical action as indicated. Don't forget to circle the action verb you use!

1. physical _____

2. mental   _____

3. physical _____

Grammaropolis

Transitive Action Verbs

Franklin <u>ate</u> his lunch at school.

Sandra <u>**memorized**</u> her notes before the big test.

Pro Tip:
A *transitive action verb* passes its action on to the object of the verb.

Let's Practice!

Instructions:
Circle the transitive action verb in each sentence and draw an arrow to its object.

EXAMPLE:
Allison (threw) a perfect pass and (won) the game.

1. Peter followed the man down the street.

2. Marita saved her birthday money.

3. Sometimes Julie makes enormous sandwiches.

4. The dragon destroyed the knights with a breath of fire.

5. I burned my toast this morning!

Your turn!

Instructions:
Write sentences with the verbs below as transitive action verbs. Don't forget to circle the verbs and draw arrows to their objects.

1. catch _____

2. eat _____

3. watch _____

Intransitive Action Verbs

Joshunda **_sprinted_** all the way down the field. When she finally **_stopped_**, she **_rested_**.

Pro Tip:
An **intransitive action verb** is an action verb that does not pass its action to an object.

Let's Practice!

Instructions:
Circle the intransitive action verb in each of the following sentences.

EXAMPLE:
The crowd (cheered) loudly as the game (ended.)

1. Children never lie to their teachers.

2. I apologized to my sister's best friend.

3. Florence spoke loudly at the meeting.

4. Henry and his classmates strolled down the street.

5. The temperature rose all morning.

Your turn!

Instructions:
Write sentences using the verbs below as intransitive action verbs. Don't forget to circle the action verbs in the sentences!

1. yell _____

2. listen _____

3. fly _____

Grammaropolis

Linking Verbs Express a State of Being

Linking verbs express a state of being. They "link" the subject to information that renames the subject.

"To be":
I **was** confused.
You **are** a teacher.

Not "to be":
You **seem** pleased.
I **feel** tired.

Pro Tip:
Linking verbs often take a form of the verb "**to be**" but they don't have to!

Let's practice!

Instructions:
Circle the linking verb in each of the following sentences.

EXAMPLE:
That restaurant (is) the most expensive one in the city.

1. Marcia's dog appeared hungry last night.

2. Your mother's voice sounds very soothing.

3. Andy and Darlene were so silly after the party.

4. That box looks heavy.

5. Some kinds elephants are larger than others.

Your turn!

Instructions:
Write three sentences using your own linking verbs. Make sure one of the sentences uses a linking verb that is not a form of "to be." Don't forget to circle the linking verbs!

1. _____

2. _____

3. _____

Action Verb or Linking Verb?

Linking Verb:
Cheo's milkshake <u>tasted</u> too sweet!

Action Verb:
Cheo <u>tasted</u> too much sugar in his milkshake.

Pro Tip:
Some words can be action verbs or linking verbs depending on how they're used.

Let's practice!

Instructions:
Circle the verb in each of the following sentences and indicate whether it is an action verb or a linking verb.

EXAMPLE:

That plant (grew) two inches in one night.   _action verb_

1. My parents finally grew tired of my attitude.   _____

2. Anna remained in the classroom after class.   _____

3. Eddie remained calm during the storm.   _____

4. I smell burning wood somewhere!   _____

5. My puppy, Mr. Pickles, smells clean and fresh after a bath.   _____

Your turn!

Instructions:
Write sentences using the verbs below as action verbs or linking verbs as indicated. Don't forget to circle the verb in the sentence!

1. look (action) _____

2. look (linking) _____

3. feel (action) _____

Irregular Past Tense Verbs

Dalton **came** to my party yesterday.
The professor **spoke** for three hours straight.
Blake **spent** all his money on cotton candy.

come → came
speak → spoke
spend → spent

Pro Tip:
An irregular past tense verb is a past tense verb that is not formed by putting -d or -ed after the present tense verb.

Let's practice!

Instructions:
Circle the correct form of the past tense verb in parentheses.

EXAMPLE:

The kids down the street (finded, found) buried treasure!

1. The little girl (built, builded) an enormous castle out of legos.

2. I (maked, made) a silly mistake on the test.

3. As son as the movie ended, we (ran, runned) out of the theater.

4. It's as though you never (heard, heared) a word I said.

5. My platypus (stealed, stole) the cupcake right off the dinner table.

Your turn!

Instructions:
Write down the correct past tense verb form for each of the present tense verbs below.

catch _____   freeze _____   take _____

lose _____   throw _____   say _____

find _____   write _____   sleep _____

Writing with Verbs

INSTRUCTIONS (PART ONE):
Brainstorm some of your favorite action verbs and linking verbs. Make different lists for action verbs that express physical action and action verbs that express mental action.

PHYSICAL ACTION VERB	MENTAL ACTION VERB	LINKING VERB
-----------------------------	-----------------------------	-----------------------------
-----------------------------	-----------------------------	-----------------------------
-----------------------------	-----------------------------	-----------------------------
-----------------------------	-----------------------------	-----------------------------

INSTRUCTIONS (PART TWO):
Now choose TWO verbs from each of your categories and use them to write a short story. Don't forget to circle the verbs!

_____

_____

_____

_____

_____

_____

_____

The Big Verb Quiz!

Name:

INSTRUCTIONS: Indicate whether the <u>underlined verb</u> below is an action verb or a linking verb.

1. The battlefield <u>appears</u> deserted even though we know the soldiers are out there.
   ○ action verb   ○ linking verb

2. Jason <u>looked</u> up at the sky to see if it was going to rain.
   ○ action verb   ○ linking verb

3. Would you please <u>smell</u> this milk? I am afraid that it is spoiled.
   ○ action verb   ○ linking verb

4. After studying all night for the test, Evan <u>looked</u> absolutely exhausted.
   ○ action verb   ○ linking verb

5. The kindergarten teacher <u>grew</u> frustrated when the children wouldn't listen.
   ○ action verb   ○ linking verb

INSTRUCTIONS: Indicate whether the <u>underlined action verb</u> below is transitive or intransitive.

6. I <u>apologized</u> even though I'm not sure I did anything wrong.
   ○ transitive   ○ intransitive

7. Vanessa <u>smiled</u> when a butterfly landed on her fingertip.
   ○ transitive   ○ intransitive

8. If you want to bake a cake, you <u>need</u> more eggs, flour, and sugar.
   ○ transitive   ○ intransitive

9. Francine's husband <u>lived</u> in Madagascar for years before moving to Kansas.
   ○ transitive   ○ intransitive

10. Have you see the ghost that <u>haunts</u> the theater?
    ○ transitive   ○ intransitive

Meet the Adjectives!

I am an adjective!

I can modify a noun or a pronoun.

I tell what kind, which one, how many, or how much.

EXAMPLES

WHAT KIND: Peter bought me a <u>**green**</u> umbrella.

WHICH ONE: Please sit in the <u>**back**</u> seat.

HOW MANY: Lee Ann wrote <u>**thirteen**</u> letters.

HOW MUCH: Ask the teacher to give us <u>**less**</u> homework.

Identifying Adjectives

The **tall** **green** trees grew along the **deserted** highway.

The **nine** puppies ate **more** food today.

Pro Tip:
An adjective modifies one or more nouns or pronouns. It can tell **what kind, which one, how many** (a number or quantity) or **how much** (an amount).

Let's Practice!

Instructions:
Circle all the adjectives in the following sentences.

EXAMPLE:
A (small) (red) light flashes whenever the camera takes a (nighttime) picture.

1. The brief conversation resulted in more rules and fewer privileges.

2. I jumped across the wide creek to the other side.

3. All students please come to the new library for a quick talk.

4. Mary read a long book about a little lamb.

5. Anita tossed her wrinkled clothes into the empty hamper.

Your turn!

Instructions:
Write sentences using more than one adjective in each sentence.
Don't forget to circle the adjectives!

1. _____

2. _____

3. _____

Grammaropolis

Words Adjectives Modify

Adjectives before:

The <u>bright</u> sunshine filled me with <u>genuine</u> happiness.

Adjectives after:

Kyle was very <u>gracious</u> after his team lost the game.

Pro Tip:
An adjective can come **before** or **after** the word or words it modifies.

Let's Practice!

Instructions:
Circle all of the adjectives in each of the following sentences.
Then draw an arrow from each adjective to the word it modifies.

EXAMPLE:
Nelson was (happy) when the (new) (model) car went on sale.

1. Jaxon is a good friend of mine.

2. There were seventeen people in the new bus.

3. Some children like to eat frozen bananas on a stick.

4. The purple flowers smell heavenly.

5. Pedro cooked us his favorite meal.

Your turn!

Instructions:
Write sentences using the adjectives below to describe a noun or pronoun. Circle each adjective and draw an arrow to the word it modifies.

1. sharp _____

2. cold _____

3. many _____

Grammaropolis

Demonstrative, Possessive, and Interrogative Adjectives

Pro Tip:

A *demonstrative* adjective shows whether the noun it modifies is singular or plural and whether it is near or far.

A *possessive* adjective modifies a noun, showing possession or ownership.

An *interrogative* adjective is used to ask a question about a noun.

Demonstrative:
Sammie gave me **these** balloons.

Possessive:
You should really finish **your** homework before the movie starts.

Interrogative:
Which car do you want to drive?

Let's Practice!

Instructions:
In each of the following sentences, draw an arrow from the adjective in *BOLD* to the word it modifies. Then indicate whether the adjective is demonstrative, possessive, or interrogative.

EXAMPLE:

It's hard for Tanisha to make up **her** mind about what to order.   _____possessive_____

1.   Please give me back **my** sandwich!   _____

2.   **Those** chocolate bars belong to Salvatore.   _____

3.   I wonder **what** room they will assign to us.   _____

4.   Jason always does **his** homework in the car.   _____

5.   I don't want to have anything to do with **that** guy.   _____

Your turn!

Instructions:
Write a sentence using the adjectives below as demonstrative (D), possessive (P), or interrogative (I). Circle the adjectives and draw arrows to the words they modify.

1.   those (D) _____

2.   which (I) _____

3.   your (P) _____

Comparative and Superlative Adjectives

Comparative:
When given a choice between two hamsters, I will always choose the <u>faster</u> hamster.

Superlative:
We all brought our hamsters for a big race to determine who had the <u>fastest</u> hamster in the land.

Pro Tip:
A *comparative adjective* is used to make a comparison between two nouns or pronouns.

Pro Tip:
A *superlative adjective* is used to describe the extreme quality of something and is used when talking about three or more nouns or pronouns.

Let's Practice!

Instructions:
In the sentences below, draw an arrow from the <u>underlined adjective</u> to the word it modifies. Then indicate whether the adjective is comparative or superlative.

EXAMPLE:

Molly is **<u>happier</u>** than Ivan because her cupcake has sprinkles.   _____comparative_____

1.   Talia's room is **<u>cleaner</u>** than mine.   _____

2.   Pepe has the **<u>shortest</u>** name in the class.   _____

3.   Lorenzo's dog seems **<u>bigger</u>** than it did yesterday.   _____

4.   That is the **<u>saddest</u>** clown I have ever seen.   _____

5.   Some people say that New Mexico has the **<u>best</u>** food of all.   _____

Your turn!

Instructions:
Write sentences turning the adjectives below into comparative (C) or superlative (S) adjectives as indicated. Don't forget to circle the adjectives!

1.   dark (S) _____

2.   hard (C) _____

3.   old (S) _____

4.   green (C) _____

Writing with Adjectives

INSTRUCTIONS (PART ONE):

Brainstorm a list of adjectives you might use to describe each of the nouns below.

1. room	2. box	3. person	4. feeling
----------------	----------------	----------------	----------------
----------------	----------------	----------------	----------------
----------------	----------------	----------------	----------------
----------------	----------------	----------------	----------------

INSTRUCTIONS (PART TWO):

Write a story that incorporates the nouns and adjectives above. Circle the adjectives when you use them!

_____

_____

_____

_____

_____

_____

The Big Adjective Quiz!

INSTRUCTIONS: Indicate whether the underlined adjective tells what kind, which one, how many, or how much.

1. Please take a number and sit in an open chair in the <u>front</u> row.
    ○ what kind   ○ which one   ○ how many   ○ how much

2. The campers ate <u>fresh</u> bread and cheese.
    ○ what kind   ○ which one   ○ how many   ○ how much

3. Nobody likes to see <u>green</u> mold on their bread.
    ○ what kind   ○ which one   ○ how many   ○ how much

4. Lyall ordered <u>two</u> entire chocolate cakes for my birthday party.
    ○ what kind   ○ which one   ○ how many   ○ how much

5. Two chocolate cakes was <u>more</u> cake than I could have possibly eaten.
    ○ what kind   ○ which one   ○ how many   ○ how much

INSTRUCTIONS: Identify the word the <u>underlined adjective</u> modifies from among the available options.

6. Yousef and Lyudmilla love to gather <u>wild</u> mushrooms in the dark forest.
    ○ love   ○ mushrooms   ○ forest   ○ gather

7. Kevin's mother looked so <u>angry</u> at both of us.
    ○ mother   ○ Kevin's   ○ us   ○ both

8. The end of that story is so very <u>sad</u>.
    ○ end   ○ story   ○ that   ○ very

9. The earth behind my house turns <u>red</u> after a heavy rain.
    ○ rain   ○ house   ○ earth   ○ behind

10. The <u>tiny</u> little tent at the circus is for children.
    ○ children   ○ circus   ○ tent   ○ little

Grammaropolis

Meet the Adverbs!

I am an adverb!

I modify a verb, adjective, or other adverb.

I usually end in -ly, but I don't have to.

EXAMPLES

MODIFYING A VERB: Speak <u>softly</u> and run <u>quickly</u>.

MODIFYING AN ADJECTIVE: My classmates are <u>often</u> silly.

MODIFYING ANOTHER ADVERB: Hector left the haunted house screaming <u>quite</u> loudly.

Identifying Adverbs

Modifying Verbs:
Kyle slept **soundly**.

"soundly" modifies the verb "slept" and tells how.

Modifying Adjectives:
I am **very** happy with this plan.

"very" modifies the adjective "happy" and tells to what extent (how much).

Modifying Other Adverbs:
He answered **quite** uncertainly.

"quite" modifies the adverb "uncertainly" and tells to what extent (how much).

Pro Tip:
*An **adverb** modifies a verb, adjective, or other adverb. It can tell more nouns or pronouns. It can tell **how, when, where** or **to what extent (how much)**.*

Let's Practice!

Instructions:
Circle all of the adverbs in the following sentences.

EXAMPLE:
Prudence's kitten (carefully) licked his (extremely) dirty paws.

1. I never read without a good source of light.

2. Antonia sometimes runs too quickly for me to catch up.

3. After she took a breath, her confidence returned immediately.

4. Be very careful when you walk backward toward the open door.

5. We stubbornly refused to change our minds.

Your turn!

Instructions:
Write sentences of your own using adverbs to modify verbs, adjectives, or other adverbs. Don't forget to circle the adverbs you use!

1. _____

2. _____

3. _____

Adverbs Can Tell "Where," "When," or "How"

Name:

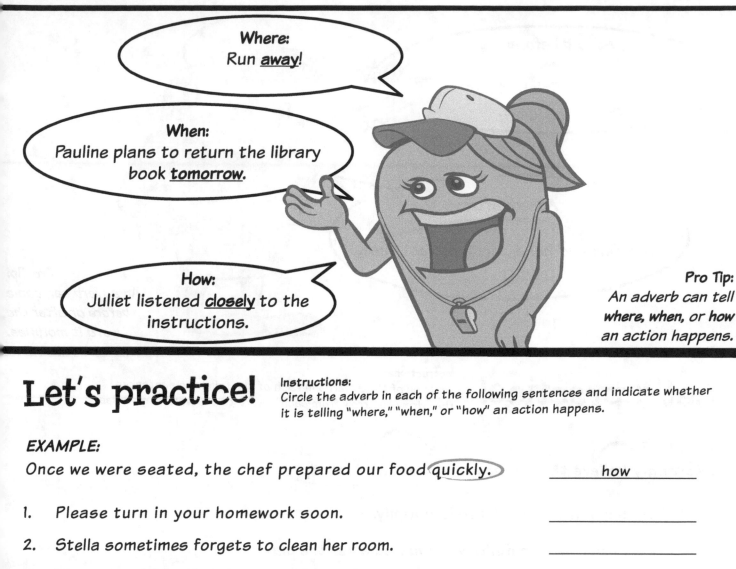

Where:
Run **away**!

When:
Pauline plans to return the library book **tomorrow**.

How:
Juliet listened **closely** to the instructions.

Pro Tip:
An adverb can tell **where, when, or how** an action happens.

Let's practice!

Instructions:
Circle the adverb in each of the following sentences and indicate whether it is telling "where," "when," or "how" an action happens.

EXAMPLE:

Once we were seated, the chef prepared our food (quickly).   _____how_____

1.   Please turn in your homework soon.   _____

2.   Stella sometimes forgets to clean her room.   _____

3.   We ran outside when it started to rain.   _____

4.   Tell Dad that I will brush my teeth later.   _____

5.   The coyote crept silently through the neighborhood.   _____

Your turn!

Instructions:
Write sentences below using adverbs to tell where, when, or how an action happens. Don't forget to circle the adverbs when you use them.

1.   where   _____

2.   when   _____

3.   how   _____

Words Adverbs Modify

Adverb before:

Sara _easily_ finished her science project.

Adverb after:

Sara finished her science project _easily_.

Pro Tip:
An adverb can come **before** or **after** the word it modifies.

Let's practice!

Instructions:
Circle all of the adverbs in each of the following sentences.
Then draw an arrow from each adverb to the word it modifies.

EXAMPLE:
I strongly believe that Bobby cheated accidentally.

1. "They are quite smart," I said happily.

2. Zeke and Sam were definitely exhausted after the play.

3. Daniela quietly sat in the corner and worked diligently.

4. Joseph told me yesterday about the homework assignment.

5. Her cat is incredibly old, so it eats very slowly.

Your turn!

Instructions:
Write sentences using the adverbs below. Circle each adverb and draw an arrow to the word it modifies.

1. loudly _____

2. soon _____

3. strongly _____

Grammaropolis

Comparative and Superlative Adverbs

Comparative:
I studied **more carefully** than you.
Henry jumped **higher** than Jake did.

Superlative:
I studied the **most carefully** of anyone.
Henry jumped the **highest** in the whole school.

Pro Tip:
A **comparative adverb** is used when comparing two people, places or things.

Pro Tip:
A **superlative adverb** indicates the extreme quality of something. It is used when talking about three or more people, places or things.

Let's Practice!

Instructions:
In each of the following sentences, draw an arrow from underlined adverb to the word it modifies. Then indicate whether the adverb is comparative or superlative.

EXAMPLE:

I arrived at school **earlier** than Billy did.   _____comparative_____

1. Pat completed the exercise the **most skillfully** of all.   _____

2. Hayden left **later** than his brother did.   _____

3. Steve's piñata broke the **most easily** out of any of them.   _____

4. Please whisper **more softly** so that you don't wake my guard dog.   _____

5. I ran to the end of the block the **fastest**.   _____

Your turn!

Instructions:
Write sentences turning the adverbs below into comparative (C) or superlative (S) adverbs as indicated. Don't forget to circle the adverb!

1. quietly (S) _____

2. sadly (C) _____

3. fast (C) _____

4. soon (S) _____

Grammaropolis

Writing with Adverbs

INSTRUCTIONS (PART ONE):
Create adverbs that tell "how" by adding -ly to the end of the adverbs below.

ADJECTIVE	ADVERB
1. _____clear_____	1. _____
2. _____strong_____	2. _____
3. _____slow_____	3. _____
4. _____glad_____	4. _____
5. _____soft_____	5. _____

INSTRUCTIONS (PART TWO):
Fill in the blanks with your favorite adverbs that tell "where" and "when."

WHERE

1. _____

2. _____

WHEN

1. _____

2. _____

INSTRUCTIONS (PART THREE):
Write a story that incorporates all of the adverbs above. Circle the adverbs when you use them!

_____

_____

_____

_____

_____

_____

The Big Adverb Quiz!

INSTRUCTIONS: Identify the adverb in each of the sentences below from the available options.

1. Aidan memorized his lines so that he could recite them backwards.
   - ○ backwards   ○ memorized   ○ that   ○ lines

2. Sit down until I finish the rest of my meal.
   - ○ finish   ○ down   ○ rest   ○ of

3. Pauline usually bikes to work, but today she decided to walk.
   - ○ bikes   ○ walk   ○ today   ○ but

4. I never wear pants, no matter how unbelievably cold it is outside.
   - ○ cold   ○ matter   ○ no   ○ never

5. The grasshopper landed softly on a bright green leaf.
   - ○ landed   ○ bright   ○ green   ○ grasshopper

INSTRUCTIONS: Indicate whether the <u>underlined adverbs</u> below tell where, when, or how.

6. Joseph's family greeted him <u>warmly</u> when he got off the plane.
   - ○ where   ○ when   ○ how

7. Kyla <u>immediately</u> knew the answer to the riddle.
   - ○ where   ○ when   ○ how

8. I have one piece of advice for you: Don't go <u>there</u>.
   - ○ where   ○ when   ○ how

9. Your friends are going to be here <u>soon</u>, so please just relax and take a seat.
   - ○ where   ○ when   ○ how

10. The bell chimed <u>loudly</u> to indicate the start of French class.
    - ○ where   ○ when   ○ how

Grammaropolis

Meet the Pronouns!

EXAMPLES

WITHOUT PRONOUNS: <u>Yasmin</u> cooked <u>a pancake breakfast</u> for <u>her brothers and sisters</u>.

WITH PRONOUNS: <u>She</u> cooked <u>it</u> for <u>them</u>.

Why We Use Pronouns

Without Pronouns:
Laura is happy because Laura bought Laura a cookie and ate the cookie for dessert.

With Pronouns:
Laura is happy because **she** bought **herself** a cookie and ate **it** for dessert.

Pro Tip:
We use pronouns so that nouns or other pronouns in the sentence don't have to be repeated.

Let's practice!

Instructions:
Fill in the blanks in the sentences below using the pronouns that make sense.

EXAMPLE:

Patricia asked if Jackie could help __*her*__ across the street.

1. Victor is a good student. _____ always does his homework.

2. Julian grabbed my shoes, put _____ on, and ran away.

3. Tasha and I signed up for the cooking class tomorrow. _____ can't wait!

4. Tomás and Frankie must love that movie because _____ can't stop talking about _____ .

5. After Bethany put on a new dress, _____ looked at _____ in the mirror.

Your turn!

Instructions:
Write a short sentence using no pronouns. Then write the same sentence replacing the nouns with pronouns. Don't forget to circle the pronouns!

_____

_____

Pronouns and Antecedents

Pro Tip:
The word (or words) that the pronoun replaces is called the antecedent.

Let's practice!

Instructions:
Circle the pronoun in each of the following sentences and draw an arrow to the word it replaces.

EXAMPLE:

Tom didn't want chocolate. He wanted vanilla.

1. Tasha swung the bat so hard that she fell down.

2. Jacob is too fast. Patricia can hardly keep up with him.

3. Is Susan going to be late for the movie? When does it start?

4. Mom and Dad are on their way. They should be here soon.

5. He and I are such good friends because we are always in the same class.

Your turn!

Instructions:
Write sentences using the word pairs below as the pronoun and antecedent. Then circle the pronoun and draw an arrow to the antecedent.

1. Baxter/he _____

2. Lucy/her _____

3. car/it _____

Subjective and Objective Pronouns

Name:

Subjective:
<u>He</u> likes bananas.
<u>We</u> want to listen.
<u>They</u> always laugh at my jokes.

Objective:
Give <u>him</u> a banana.
Please listen to <u>us</u>.
Leonard is laughing at <u>them</u>.

Pro Tip:
A subjective pronoun acts as the **subject** of the sentence.

Pro Tip:
An objective pronoun acts as the **object** of the sentence.

Let's Practice!

Instructions:
Circle the pronoun in each of the sentences below and indicate whether it is subjective or objective pronoun.

EXAMPLE:

Devin doesn't think that bacon is good for (me.)   ___objective___

1. It shouldn't be too long now.   _____

2. Are they going to run a marathon?   _____

3. Running a marathon would be hard for them.   _____

4. Steven promised to give you an expensive gift.   _____

5. Well, this certainly feels like an odd thing to say.   _____

Your turn!

Instructions:
Write sentences using the pronouns below. Circle the pronouns when you use them and write S for subjective and O for objective above the circles.

1. her   _____

2. us   _____

3. we   _____

4. me   _____

Intensive and Reflexive Pronouns

Intensive:
You **yourself** are the biggest goofball I know.
Glenda baked that cake **herself**.

Reflexive:
Roger looked at **himself** in the mirror.
We sang **ourselves** a song.

Pro Tip:
An **intensive** pronoun emphasizes, or intensifies, a noun or another pronoun.

Pro Tip:
A **reflexive** pronoun directs the action of the verb back to the subject of the sentence.

Let's Practice!

Instructions:
In each of the following sentences, indicate whether underlined pronoun is intensive or reflexive and draw an arrow to its antecedent.

EXAMPLE:
Stuart baked the cake for **himself**.   <u>reflexive</u>

1.   Gillian told me the answer **herself**.   _____

2.   We gave **ourselves** an extra day to finish the project.   _____

3.   I **myself** feel extremely happy to be alive today.   _____

4.   Roger watched nervously as Annie gave **herself** a pep talk.   _____

5.   The kitty meowed **itself** to sleep last night.   _____

Your turn!

Instructions:
Write sentences using the pronouns below as indicated: (R) for reflexive and (I) for intensive. Circle each pronoun and draw an arrow to its antecedent.

1. himself (R)   _____

2. themselves (R)   _____

3. yourself (I)   _____

Pronoun or Adjective?

Adjective:
Jeanette is happy because <u>her</u> sister is home for the weekend.

Pronoun:
Jeanette's sister gave <u>her</u> a big hug.

Pro Tip:
Some words can be either pronouns or adjectives, depending on how they're used in the sentence.

Let's Practice!

Instructions:
Indicate whether the <u>underlined word</u> is an adjective or a pronoun. If it is an adjective, draw an arrow to the word it modifies. If it is a pronoun, draw an arrow to the word it replaces.

EXAMPLE:

I want <u>**some**</u> cheese for breakfast!   ___adjective___

1. <u>**This**</u> is not the correct answer.   _____

2. <u>**That**</u> answer is incorrect.   _____

3. Tammy told Bethany that <u>**her**</u> handwriting is messy.   _____

4. I like mashed potatoes. Do you have <u>**any**</u> left?   _____

5. Are there <u>**any**</u> other fans of mashed potatoes here?   _____

Your turn!

Instructions:
Write sentences using the words below as indicated: (A) for adjective and (P) for pronoun. Don't forget to circle the word in each sentence.

1. her (P) _____

2. that (A) _____

3. those (P) _____

4. some (A) _____

Writing with Pronouns

INSTRUCTIONS (PART ONE):
Write a short story without using any pronouns at all. You might feel the urge to use pronouns so that your writing doesn't seem awkward (especially toward the end of the story), but control yourself! No pronouns!

_____

_____

_____

_____

_____

INSTRUCTIONS (PART TWO):
Write the same short story, but this time, replace ALL of the nouns in the story with pronouns. This means that you will have an entire story WITHOUT antecedents!

_____

_____

_____

_____

INSTRUCTIONS (PART THREE):
That second story probably didn't make any sense at all because without antecedents, you couldn't figure out what the pronouns were replacing! Now rewrite the story one more time using a nice mix of pronouns and antecedents to make your writing clear.

_____

_____

_____

_____

Grammaropolis

The Big Pronoun Quiz!

INSTRUCTIONS: Identify the antecedent (the word the <u>underlined pronoun</u> replaces) from the options below.

1. To save money, the Gemini family cut their own hair <u>themselves</u>.
○ money ○ Gemini ○ family ○ hair

2. Antonio asked his wife to take a picture of <u>him</u> in the garden.
○ his ○ picture ○ Antonio ○ garden

3. The sunflowers lifted their faces to the sky as if to say, "The sun is smiling on <u>us</u>."
○ faces ○ sunflowers ○ sun ○ sky

4. Parents work hard for their children because they want happiness for <u>them</u>.
○ children ○ Parents ○ they ○ happiness

5. When Charles awoke from his nap in the woods, <u>he</u> had no idea where he was.
○ he ○ his ○ Charles ○ nap

INSTRUCTIONS: Indicate whether the <u>underlined pronouns</u> below are reflexive or intensive.

6. We give <u>ourselves</u> a hard time when we don't exercise daily
○ reflexive ○ intensive

7. I know I am safe because I locked the door <u>myself</u>.
○ reflexive ○ intensive

8. Anti-virus software helps the computer clean <u>itself</u>.
○ reflexive ○ intensive

9. Samuel learned how to sew because he wants to alter his clothes <u>himself</u>.
○ reflexive ○ intensive

10. On rainy days, Robin entertains <u>herself</u> by reading about chocolate factories.
○ reflexive ○ intensive

Grammaropolis

Meet the Conjunctions!

EXAMPLES

JOINING WORDS: Billy **and** Joaquin played basketball this morning.

JOINING PHRASES: I usually keep my treasures under the bed **or** in a box.

JOINING CLAUSES: Nelson's platypus won't bite, **so** you can pet him!

Coordinating Conjunctions

Words:
Albert likes
peas **and** carrots.

Phrases:
Do you exercise in the
morning **or** at night?

Complete Thoughts:
Those pickles are expensive,
but I ordered some anyway

Pro Tip:
The FANBOYS (also known as coordinating conjunctions) are used to join **words, phrases,** or **complete thoughts** (independent clauses).

Let's practice!

Instructions:
Circle all of the coordinating conjunctions in the sentences below.

EXAMPLE:
Frankie is tired (and) cranky, (so) we should let him sleep.

1. Traci doesn't enjoy stew, nor does she like pasta and meatballs.

2. Dogs shed a lot, but that's okay with me!

3. I get plenty of sleep, yet I still feel so tired.

4. Sir Patrick is a good role model, for he behaves properly at all times.

5. Lexi and her mother came over for dinner but ended up spending the night.

Your turn!

Instructions:
Write sentences using the following conjunctions to join words or word groups.
Don't forget to circle the conjunction in the sentence!

1. but _____

2. and _____

3. so _____

Grammaropolis

Correlative Conjunctions

Either you give me ice cream **or** I will cry.

Both my little sister **and** my elderly grandmother are fans of the Disney channel.

Pro Tip:
A **correlative** conjunction is a two-part conjunction used to join words or phrases used in the same way.

Pro Tip:
Common correlative conjunctions are **either/or, neither/nor, whether/or,** and **not only/but also.**

Let's Practice!

Instructions:
Circle both parts of the correlative conjunction in each of the following sentences and draw a line linking the two parts..

EXAMPLE:
Neither the Astros nor the Rockies won the World Series last year.

1. Whether we drive or we fly, we are going to get there safely.

2. Tallulah is not only very tall but also extremely fast.

3. My day included trips to both the grocery store and the gas station

4. Either you give me a piece of chocolate or I will steal it from you when you're sleeping.

5. Both the living room and the dining room are messy.

Your turn!

Instructions:
Write complete sentences using the correlative conjunctions below. Don't forget to circle and link both parts!

1. either/or _____

2. both/and _____

3. neither/nor _____

Grammaropolis

Subordinating Conjunctions

Subordinate Clause First:
<u>Wherever</u> my brother goes, he likes to whistle.

<u>Because</u> it rained so hard, the streets flooded.

Subordinate Clause Second:
My brother likes to whistle <u>**wherever**</u> he goes.

The streets were flooded <u>**because**</u> it rained so hard.

Pro Tip:
A **subordinating conjunction** introduces a subordinate, or dependent, clause.

Pro Tip:
The subordinate clause can come before or after the independent clause.

Let's Practice!

Instructions:
Circle the subordinating conjunction in each of the following sentences and then underline the entire subordinate clause.

EXAMPLE:
(Whenever) <u>I see a clown</u>, I want to start crying.

1. Don't blame me if the food is terrible.

2. Although the party ended hours ago, people are still here.

3. While I have you on the phone, let me ask you one more question.

4. Douglas will be well rested after he takes a nap.

5. I won't go in there until I know it's safe.

Your turn!

Instructions:
Write complete sentences using each of the subordinating conjunctions below to introduce a subordinate clause. Don't forget to circle the conjunction and underline the entire subordinate clause!

1. unless _____

2. because _____

3. if _____

Identifying Conjunctions

Without Conjunctions:
I love making cookies. I love making brownies. I enjoy making cupcakes. I enjoy finding tasty recipes. I enjoy learning them.

With Conjunctions:
I love making cookies, brownies, **and** cupcakes **because** I enjoy finding **and** learning tasty recipes.

Pro Tip:
Conjunctions make it possible to link words and ideas together in many different ways.

Let's Practice!

Instructions:
Circle all of the conjunctions in each of the following sentences.

EXAMPLE:
Molly asked for milk (and) sugar, (for) she does not enjoy black coffee.

1. If you give me enough time, I will iron your pants and shirt.

2. After we eat, we won't be hungry anymore.

3. The dogs and cats barked and meowed, so we let them inside.

4. Do you want cake or pie for dessert?

5. Whenever I hear that noise, I scream and run in the opposite direction.

Your turn!

Instructions:
Write sentences that incorporate each of the words below as conjunctions. Don't forget to circle the conjunctions!

1. because _____

2. and _____

3. or _____

Writing with Conjunctions

INSTRUCTIONS (PART ONE):

Circle THREE coordinating conjunctions, TWO correlative conjunctions, and TWO subordinating conjunctions from among the choices below.

COORDINATING

for
and
nor
but
or
yet
so

CORRELATIVE

either/or
neither/nor
not only/but also
both/and
whether/or

SUBORDINATING

after	even if	though
although	even though	unless
as	if	until
because	now that	whenever
before	once	wherever
by the time	since	while
	so	

INSTRUCTIONS (PART TWO):

Now write a story that incorporates the conjunctions you have circled. Remember to circle the conjunctions once you use them in the story as well!

_____

_____

_____

_____

_____

_____

_____

Grammaropolis

The Big Conjunction Quiz!

Name: _____

INSTRUCTIONS: Indicate the correct type of conjunction for each of the <u>underlined conjunctions</u> below.

1. Nicholas eats a lot of vegetables, <u>for</u> he wants to be healthy.
   ○ coordinating   ○ correlative   ○ subordinating

2. Billy fears <u>neither</u> vampires and werewolves <u>nor</u> dragons and unicorns.
   ○ coordinating   ○ correlative   ○ subordinating

3. Mason isn't allowed to call his friends <u>until</u> he finishes his homework.
   ○ coordinating   ○ correlative   ○ subordinating

4. <u>As soon as</u> the movie ended, I burst into tears.
   ○ coordinating   ○ correlative   ○ subordinating

5. Crepes are usually sweet, <u>but</u> some recipes call veggies, meat, or cheese.
   ○ coordinating   ○ correlative   ○ subordinating

6. You can order me <u>either</u> a hamburger <u>or</u> a hot dog, but I don't want any fries.
   ○ coordinating   ○ correlative   ○ subordinating

7. Sasha feels proud of herself <u>when</u> she gets her work done on time.
   ○ coordinating   ○ correlative   ○ subordinating

8. The best students <u>not only</u> study hard <u>but also</u> work together.
   ○ coordinating   ○ correlative   ○ subordinating

9. Gerald arrived earlier than he'd planned, <u>yet</u> he still missed the first act!
   ○ coordinating   ○ correlative   ○ subordinating

10. <u>Although</u> they disagree about politics, Charles and Kathy still respect each other.
    ○ coordinating   ○ correlative   ○ subordinating

Grammaropolis

Meet the Prepositions!

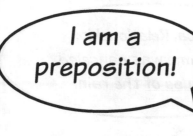

I am a preposition!

I show the relationship between the object (a noun or pronoun) and other words in the sentence.

I help tell where or when something happens.

EXAMPLES

WHERE: Meet me <u>**next to**</u> the stop sign <u>**down**</u> the street.

WHEN: I will do my homework <u>**after**</u> dinner <u>**on**</u> Sunday.

LOGICAL: The dog <u>**with**</u> the blue collar is mine.

Identifying Prepositions

Space (where):
I left a key <u>under</u> the welcome mat.

Time (when):
I never eat <u>during</u> class.

Logical Relationship:
The game was canceled <u>because of</u> the rain.

Pro Tip:
A preposition locates an object in **time** or **space** or shows a **logical relationship** between the object and the rest of the sentence.

Pro Tip:
A preposition that is more than one word but acts as a single preposition is called a **compound preposition.** Examples include: **next to, instead of, because of,** and **due to.**

Let's practice!

Instructions:
Circle the prepositions in the following sentences and then indicate whether they help tell when or where the action of the verb happens or if they show a logical relationship. Don't forget to look for compound prepositions!

EXAMPLE:

Someone should give me medicine (for) my cold.   _logical_

1. The owl hooted as it flew above the forest.   _____

2. It's the most wonderful time of the year.   _____

3. In my wallet you will find my driver's license.   _____

4. The old dog ate wet food instead of dry food   _____

5. I promise that I will make pancakes in the morning.   _____

Your turn!

Instructions:
Finish the sentences below by incorporating your own prepositions. Don't forget to circle the prepositions!

1. <u>Sandra bought a ticket</u> _____

2. <u>Annie and Sammie read</u> _____

3. <u>The library is open</u> _____

Grammaropolis

Prepositional Phrases

A preposition is placed at the beginning of a prepositional phrase.

next to the couch

outside the teachers' lounge

Pro Tip:
A prepositional phrase starts with a preposition and ends with the object of the preposition.

Let's practice!

Instructions:
In each of the following sentences, underline the entire prepositional phrase and circle the preposition. There may be more than one!

EXAMPLE:
Jana came home at the exact time I was leaving.

1. I never drink hot cocoa without marshmallows.

2. Charlie fell asleep in his brand new purple bed.

3. I hid under the kitchen table during the lightning storm.

4. Vanessa hopped like a bunny instead of a frog.

5. Due to my bad memory, I forgot that guy's name.

Your turn!

Instructions:
Write sentences that incorporate the prepositional phrases below. Remember to underline the prepositional phrases and circle the prepositions.

1. around the room _____

2. like a bee _____

3. after dinner _____

Preposition or Adverb?

Adverb:
We ran <u>around</u>.
"around" is by itself, without the rest of a phrase. That means it's an adverb.

Preposition:
We ran <u>around the field</u>.
"around the field" is a prepositional phrase, so around is a preposition.

Pro Tip:
Some words can be used as either prepositions or adverbs. Remember that a preposition always has to be at the front of the phrase. If there's no phrase, it's not a preposition!

Let's Practice!

Instructions:
Indicate whether the <u>underlined word</u> is a preposition or an adverb. If it is a preposition, draw an arrow to the object of the phrase. If it is an adverb, draw an arrow to the word it modifies.

EXAMPLE:

When I fell <u>**down**</u>, I started crying in pain.   _____adverb_____

1.   I fell <u>**down**</u> the stairs and hurt my knee!   _____

2.   Will someone please take the trash <u>**outside**</u>?   _____

3.   If you look <u>**outside**</u> the window, you will see a lot of trash.   _____

4.   Move <u>**along**</u>. There's nothing to see here.   _____

5.   Valerie and her little sister planted flowers <u>**along**</u> the path.   _____

Your turn!

Instructions:
Write sentences using the words below as adverbs (A) or prepositions (P) as indicated. If it is a preposition, draw an arrow to the object of the phrase. If it is an adverb, draw an arrow to the word it modifies.

1. out (A) _____

2. by (P) _____

3. up (P) _____

4. up (A) _____

Writing with Prepositions

INSTRUCTIONS (PART ONE):

Create six prepositional phrases with the prepositions below. Be sure to use at least one compound preposition.

SINGLE WORD PREPOSITIONS					COMPOUND PREPOSITIONS
above	behind	down	near	through	according to
across	below	during	off	throughout	ahead of
after	beneath	from	on	to	apart from
against	beside	in	out	toward	due to
around	between	inside	outside	under	because of
at	beyond	into	over	until	next to
before	by		since	upon	resulting in

1._____   4._____

2._____   5._____

3._____   6._____

INSTRUCTIONS (PART TWO):

Now write a story that incorporates the prepositions you have circled. Remember to circle the prepositions once you use them in the story as well!

_____

_____

_____

_____

_____

_____

Grammaropolis

The Big Preposition Quiz!

INSTRUCTIONS: Indicate whether the <u>underlined prepositions</u> below help tell where, when, or show a logical relationship.

1. The man was not old, yet he walked <u>with</u> a cane.
   O where   O when   O logical relationship

2. The cat burglar crept <u>along</u> the mansion's stone portico.
   O where   O when   O logical relationship

3. Felicia helps read children's stories <u>at</u> her local public library.
   O where   O when   O logical relationship

4. The students must wear blue blazers <u>because of</u> the school dress code.
   O where   O when   O logical relationship

5. I always wake up <u>before</u> the rooster.
   O where   O when   O logical relationship

INSTRUCTIONS: Indicate whether the <u>underlined words</u> below are prepositions or an adverbs.

6. As Harriet was walking into the library, her best friend was walking <u>out</u>.
   O preposition   O adverb

7. That particular kind of flower only grows <u>on</u> the tops of tall mountains.
   O preposition   O adverb

8. The chorus started singing as the lights went <u>down</u>.
   O preposition   O adverb

9. The lonely old woman just wanted other people to be <u>around</u>.
   O preposition   O adverb

10. The even lonelier old man just wanted to be <u>around</u> other people.
    O preposition   O adverb

Grammaropolis

Meet the Interjections!

EXAMPLES

MILD EMOTION: <u>Gee</u>, you really seem friendly.

STRONG EMOTION: <u>Yay</u>! I just wont the lottery!

Identifying Interjections

Mild Emotion:
<u>Hey</u>, can I borrow a mechanical pencil?

Strong Emotion:
<u>Hey</u>! That's my mechanical pencil!

Pro Tip:
Mild emotion is set apart with a **comma**.
Strong emotion is set apart with an **exclamation mark**.

Let's practice!

Instructions:
Circle the interjection in each of the following sentences and indicate whether it is expressing mild or strong emotion.

EXAMPLE:

(Um,) I think that was my idea.   <u>mild</u>

1. "Eureka!" he said. "Now I understand."   _____

2. Eeek! I just saw a mouse!   _____

3. Wow, those pants are pretty expensive.   _____

4. Yeah! My team finally won a game.   _____

5. Ahh, that hot cocoa really hits the spot.   _____

Your turn!

Instructions:
Write sentences using the interjections below to express mild or strong emotion, as indicated.

1. C'mon (mild) _____

2. Yikes (strong) _____

3. Oh (strong) _____

Writing with Interjections

Name:

INSTRUCTIONS (PART ONE):

Write down ten interjections you might use to express mild or strong emotion. Feel free to make up a few of them if you want! Circle your six favorite ones.

1._____   6._____

2._____   7._____

3._____   8._____

4._____   9._____

5._____   10._____

INSTRUCTIONS (PART TWO):

Now write sentences using your favorite interjections. Remember to use a comma when you express mild emotion and an exclamation mark with strong emotion!

MILD EMOTION

1. _____

2. _____

3. _____

STRONG EMOTION:

1. _____

2. _____

3. _____

Grammaropolis

The Big Interjection Quiz!

Name:

INSTRUCTIONS: Identify the interjection in each of the sentences below from among the available options.

1. Ay! I almost just dropped the vase!

   ○ dropped   ○ almost   ○ Ay   ○ vase

2. Boy, that singer sure can sing!

   ○ that   ○ Boy   ○ sing   ○ sure

3. Ew, I'll pass. I never put anchovies in my cereal.

   ○ Ew   ○ never   ○ pass   ○ my

4. "Ouch!" yelped the carpenter. "I just hit my thumb with the hammer!"

   ○ yelped   ○ Ouch   ○ hit   ○ hammer

5. I think I figured out what the problem is. Eureka!

   ○ think   ○ what   ○ Eureka   ○ problem

INSTRUCTIONS: Indicate whether the <u>underlined interjections</u> below express mild emotion or strong emotion.

6. <u>C'mon!</u> That was a foul!

   ○ mild emotion   ○ strong emotion

7. <u>Oh</u>, I know what you're trying to say.

   ○ mild emotion   ○ strong emotion

8. <u>Yeah</u>, I'm going to have to go ahead and tell you not to climb the railing like that.

   ○ mild emotion   ○ strong emotion

9. <u>Boo hoo</u>! My favorite band broke up!

   ○ mild emotion   ○ strong emotion

10. <u>Ha ha</u>, that's so funny, I forgot to laugh.

   ○ mild emotion   ○ strong emotion

Grammaropolis

The Big Quiz Answer Key!

NOUNS

1. collective	6. singular
2. compound	7. plural
3. abstract	8. singular
4. compound	9. plural
5. proper	10. plural

PRONOUNS

1. family	6. reflexive
2. Antonio	7. intensive
3. sunflowers	8. intensive
4. children	9. intensive
5. word	10. reflexive

VERBS

1. linking verb	6. intransitive
2. action verb	7. intransitive
3. action verb	8. transitive
4. linking verb	9. intransitive
5. linking verb	10. transitive

CONJUNCTIONS

1. coordinating	6. correlative
2. correlative	7. subordinating
3. subordinating	8. correlative
4. subordinating	9. coordinating
5. coordinating	10. subordinating

ADJECTIVES

1. which one	6. mushrooms
2. what kind	7. mother
3. what kind	8. end
4. how many	9. earth
5. how much	10. tent

PREPOSITIONS

1. logical	6. adverb
2. where	7. preposition
3. where	8. adverb
4. logical	9. adverb
5. when	10. preposition

ADVERBS

1. backwards	6. how
2. down	7. when
3. today	8. where
4. never	9. when
5. bright	10. how

INTERJECTIONS

1. Ay	6. strong
2. Boy	7. mild
3. Ew	8. mild
4. Ouch	9. strong
5. Eureka	10. mild

GRAMMAR CURRICULUM CHECKLIST

THE STORYBOOKS

4/24/2019 | $6.99
Paperback | 32 pages | 8" x 8"
Full-color illustrations throughout
Includes instructional back matter
Ages 7 to 11 | Grades 1 to 5
JUVENILE NONFICTION /
LANGUAGE ARTS / GRAMMAR

9781644420157 | Noun
9781644420171 | Verb
9781644420133 | Adjective
9781644420102 | Adverb
9781644420164 | Pronoun
9781644420119 | Conjunction
9781644420140 | Preposition
9781644420126 | Interjection

- An eight-book series starring the parts of speech, which are personified based on the roles they play in the sentence.

- Featuring a different character-based adventure for every part of speech.

- Each book includes standards–aligned definitions and examples, just like you'd find in a textbook (but way more fun).

THE WORKBOOKS

3/03/2020 | $12.99 | B&W
PB | 64 pages | 11"H x 8.5"W
Includes quizzes & instruction
Ages 7 to 11 | Grades 1 to 5
JUVENILE NONFICTION /
LANGUAGE ARTS / GRAMMAR

9781644420300 | Grade 1
9781644420317 | Grade 2
9781644420324 | Grade 3
9781644420331 | Grade 4
9781644420188 | Grade 5

- Skill-building workbooks featuring character-based instruction along with various comprehension checks and writing exercises.

- Aligned to Common Core and state standards for K–5.

Grammaropolis is available through Ingram Publisher Services.
Contact your IPS Sales Representative to order.
Call (866) 400-5351, Fax (800) 838-1149, ips@ingramcontent.com, or visit ipage.

Printed in the USA
CPSIA information can be obtained
at www.ICGtesting.com
JSHW060239160824
68134JS00058BA/2679